THE BASICS OF
WINNING
VIDEO
POKER

THE BASICS OF
WINNING
VIDEO
POKER

J. Edward Allen

- Gambling Research Institute -
Cardoza Publishing

Fourth Edition

Copyright ©1985, 1992, 1998, 2002 by Cardoza Publishing
- All Rights Reserved -

ISBN: 1-58042-067-2
Library of Congress Catalog No: 2002105879

Visit our new web site or write us
for a full list of Cardoza books and strategies.

CARDOZA PUBLISHING

PO Box 1500 Cooper Station, New York, NY 10276
Phone (800)577-WINS
email: cardozapub@aol.com
www.cardozapub.com

Table of Contents

Tables & Charts

1. Introduction

Video poker has become the most popular game played not only in gambling casinos and clubs, but also in bars, drugstores, supermarkets, gas stations and anyplace else where these machines can be fitted into a vacant space. Their popularity is enormous, for the screen shows five cards from a deck, and the player will get payoffs depending on the final hand. In essence, it's draw poker played electronically.

And the beauty of the game is that it can be beaten and can be played skillfully, unlike the slot machines in which no skill is necessary. When you play video poker, you will be rewarded for correct play, and we'll show you in this book just how to do this.

Having skill at this game pays off, not only in continual wins, but in jackpots as well. The jackpots can be lucrative, in the thousands of dollars for the quarter and dollar machines.

Playing correctly and picking the right machines to gamble at, makes this game almost an even-up match with the casino.

In this book, we're going to introduce you to the fascinating world of video poker, showing you all the games available to play, and which ones are best to risk money at. If you follow our advice and play intelligently and sanely, you're going to end up a winner!

2. How to Play Video Poker

Introduction to Poker Hands

We'll briefly show the various hands you can be dealt, in descending order of strength, with the best hand listed first.

POKER HANDS
Royal Flush - A K Q J 10 of the same suit.
Straight Flush – Any five-card sequence in the same suit, such as J 10 9 8 7. Also A 2 3 4 5.
Four of a Kind – All four cards of the same rank such as 7 7 7 7.
Full House – Three of a kind combined with a pair, such as 4 4 4 Q Q.
Flush – Any five cards of the same suit, but not in sequence.
Straight – Five cards in sequence, but not of the same suit, such as Q J 10 9 8. Also A 2 3 4 5.
Three of a Kind – Three cards of the same rank, with two odd cards, such as K K K 7 2.
Two Pair – Two separate pairs plus an odd card, such as 9 9 5 5 J.
One High Pair – Any pair Jacks or better, with three odd cards, such as A A 9 6 4.
One Low Pair – Any pair below Jacks, with three odd cards, such as 5 5 K Q J.
No Pair – Five odd cards.

Some machines contain wild cards, such as a deuce (2) or a Joker. With these machines, five-of-a-kind hands have big payoffs, but rank below a Royal Flush.

Video Poker is basically draw poker, with all cards dealt out by the machine's computer. Initially five cards are dealt to the player, and are shown on the screen.

The player can now improve his hand by holding certain cards and discarding others. He could hold all five cards if he was dealt a flush, for example, but discard an odd card if dealt a four-flush, such as Ace 9 8 5 of spades and a heart 3. In this instance, he would discard the 3 and hold the four spades, then draw for a possible improvement of his hand.

If he is dealt a spade, he would have a flush and be paid off. If he was dealt another Ace, he'd have a pair of Aces, a high pair, and be paid off for that hand. Another 9 8 or 5 wouldn't help because it's a low pair, below Jacks, and this hand would be a loser.

Let's follow another hand, and suppose that a player has received the following initial cards:

♠Q ♦7 ♣Q ♠3 ♥6

She has been dealt a pair of queens, which she will hold, while discarding the rest of the cards. Under each card on the player's keyboard is a **hold button**, which, when pressed, will hold the card above it. If a player makes a mistake and presses this button incorrectly, by pressing it again, the **hold** disappears.

So now the two queens are held, and the 7, 3 and 6 will be discarded and replaced by three new cards. Let's assume that the player's hand looks like this after the draw:

♠Q ♥Q ♣Q ♠K ♦4

She has improved her hand to Three-of-a-Kind, which means a bigger payout than the pair of queens. The stronger the final poker hand, if it qualifies for a payout, the bigger the payout.

The machine deals out cards from a 52 card deck, and will never deal a card previously discarded on the same hand. Thus, if a player gets rid of the 6 of clubs, he can't get it back after the draw.

The final hand determines whether or not the player has won or lost. The board will flash **Winner** and sometimes show the kind of winning hand by flashing **Flush**, for instance. If the hand ended up as a losing hand, nothing will be flashed on the screen.

An important consideration, one that should always be kept in mind by the player, is that, although this is draw poker, it is not being played against other players. It is played against the machine, and all one has to do is get hands sufficient to be paid off.

A mistake many experienced draw poker players make is thinking they have to beat other players. They'll retain an Ace as a **kicker** with a small pair. That may be good play against other players, but it is a mistake in video poker. By holding the Ace they're taking away a spot for a card that can help the 9s possibly become three 9s or four 9s.

Or they'll discard a pair of 3s, thinking they're weak. They are weak but can improve, and it's much better to start with them than a blank screen, getting five new cards.

In regular draw poker, played against other players, it wouldn't pay to hold a small pair, but often, as we shall see later, it's the best play in Video Poker. Always keep in mind that you want to be paid off by the machine, not other players, and therefore, you'll have to alter your strategy to this effect.

Step by Step Play

When Video Poker machines were first introduced, it was necessary to start play by inserting coins into them. If you won a payout, you'd be rewarded with credits, which you could play off. When you ran out of credits, you'd have to put coins back in. Doing this slowed down the game considerably.

Today, to start the machine, you simply place a bill into a slot, either a $1, $5, $10, $20 or $100 bill, and once the machine scans and accepts the bill, credits flash on the machine. On a quarter machine, putting in $20 gives you 80 credits. A $100 bill gives you 400 credits.

On the machine are buttons which are simple to operate and understand. You can bet the maximum five credits by pushing a button that states "maximum credits." Or you can play one credit or more by pushing a button that states "one credit." Each time you push this button, another credit shows up to five.

We strongly suggest that you always play the maximum number of credits in order to possibly hit the best payout on Royal Flushes.

If you had put a $20 bill into a quarter machine, you can play out the 80 credits, five at a time. Thus, you are able to play much much faster. Once you press the maximum credit button, five cards will show on the screen, dealt in sequence. After examining the five cards of this hand, you can retain or discard whatever card or cards will give you the best chance at a payout.

On the screen, at the same time, you'll see the various payouts that you can get, from a pair of jacks or better all the way up to a Royal

Flush.

To hold the cards you want to keep, you simply press the **hold button** under that particular card. On some modern machines you can touch the card on the screen to hold it. If you mistakenly press the hold button, by pressing it again, it will no longer be held.

Let's assume that your dealt cards are as follows:

♦3 ♥6 ♣7 ♠10 ♥10

The best chances to win are to hold the two 10s, and to discard the other cards. A pair of 10s won't give you a payout but they can improve all the way from two pair to four of a kind. You now press the hold button under each 10 and "held" will appear under each 10 on the screen. Here's what the screen will now look like:

♦3   ♥6   ♣7   ♠10   ♥10
                HELD HELD

Now that you're satisfied with your held cards, you press another button, called the **Deal/Draw** or **Deal** button. This will allow you to draw cards to the two held 10s. The 3, 6 and 7 will disappear from the screen and be replaced by the newly drawn cards. Your final hand may look like this:

♠J   ♦A   ♦J   ♠10   ♥10

You've improved to two pair, and the

screen will show **Winner - Two Pair**. On most Jacks or better machines, you will receive a credit of ten coins. Having started with 80 credits and having used 5 credits to play the hand, your credit total will now be 85.

Cashing Out

As you accumulate credits, another button on the machine will stay lit. This is the **Cashout** or **Payout** button. Whenever you want to cash out, by pressing this button, your credits will be converted into coins and will fall into the metal area that takes such coins. It will completely use up your credits as coins.

At times, if you've been extremely lucky, you may deplete all the coins in the machine. When that happens, press the **Service** button and a casino employee will come and refill the machine with coins, so you can properly cash out.

On many modern machines, you can now also get paid by ticket, rather than by coins. You simply press the **Ticket** button, and your total credits will be shown on a ticket in dollars and cents.

For example, if you had 105 credits on a quarter machine, the ticket will read $26.25.

You take this ticket to a change booth for redemption in money, or you can play it at another machine that takes tickets in lieu of bills.

Some Representative Hands

What happens if you've been dealt a complete dud, five cards that are low in value and mismatched (**rags**) so that you don't want to hold any of them? You simply press the **Deal/Draw** button and all five cards will disappear from the screen to be replaced by five different cards.

What if the five cards you've been dealt at the outset are such that you don't want to draw any cards to the hand? For example, let's assume that you've been dealt the following hand:

♦4 ♦A ♦3 ♦9 ♦8

You have five diamonds showing, a Flush, an immediate winner, without having to draw additional cards. What you do now is press the **Hold** button under each and every card shown, till there are five **HELDS** on the screen.

Then you press the **Deal/Draw** button, and you will see **Winner-Flush** show up on the screen. Some screens will also show the number of credits you've won.

If you have an immediate winner totaling five cards, such as a Flush before the draw, *you must hold all the cards to get the payoff.* If you don't press all the **Hold** buttons and simply press **Deal/Draw**, the winning cards will disappear from the screen and you'll get five fresh cards.

Now, for the ultimate win. What if you end up with a Royal Flush? You'll see **Winner-Royal Flush** on the screen. If it's a quarter machine that has a standard 4,000 coin jackpot, you'll collect that amount, but not from the machine. Lights will flash, and employees will come over quickly to verify the jackpot and pay you off in cash. Stay where you are and don't touch the machine. Guard it with your presence. If no employee shows up, ring for **Service.** A casino employee will come by.

On a progressive quarter machine, where the jackpot starts at $1,000 and goes higher with every play, you may see **Winner-Royal Flush** and the total win. Or just by looking at the progressive jackpot total on the top line, you'll see what you have won. If the win is over $1,200, you'll be asked to show ID or a social security number and you'll be handed cash along with a W-2G form to fill out and file with your income tax for that year.

When you get to a Video Poker machine, familiarize yourself with all the buttons before playing. If there's something you don't understand, ask a casino employee to explain it to you.

Now that you're ready to play Video Poker, let's move on to the most common of the machines, the one that originally made this game so popular, the Jacks or Better Video Poker machine.

3. Jacks or Better

Full Payout, Flat-Top & Progressives

Jacks or Better in Video Poker refers to a pair of Jacks, Queens, Kings or Aces. Since the Queen, King or Ace is of a higher rank than the Jack, any pair consisting of these cards is known as Jacks or Better, or a High Pair.

If you get a pair of Jacks, Queens, Kings or Aces as your final hand, five credits will be added to your total. For example, suppose you end up with a pair of Queens. You'll be declared a **Winner** and be given five credits.

Although you're not making any profit since you invested five credits in the play of the hand, these returned credits really add up and keeps you in the game, as you try for that jackpot!

Once you master Jacks or Better, you'll be able to play the other games of Video Poker more intelligently, and we'll discuss those games in future sections. But the Jacks or Better machines are the ones you're most likely to encounter, since they're the most popular of the Video Poker games.

At one time, when discussing Jacks or Better machines, we'd write about the **Full-Payout** or **Flat-Top** machine, and the **Progressive** machine. The Full-Payout or Flat-Top will pay you a fixed amount if you hit the Royal Flush – four thousand coins or credits on the quarter machines, provided that you bet all five credits, or the maximum wager.

With the Progressive machine, you'll be paid a jackpot consisting of the amount showing on the Progressive payout. This payment begins with 4,000 credits or coins or $1,000 on the quarter machines and goes up from there. So, in most cases, if you hit the Royal Flush on the Progressive 25¢ machines, you can expect to cash in from $1,000 to about $3,000 and sometimes more.

Today, there are a number of other Jacks or Better machines with varying payouts, known by such names as **Bonus, Double Bonus, Double Double Bonus** and so forth. We'll cover these machines later on. But for now, we'll concentrate on the Jacks or Better machines, both Flat Tops and Progressives, with a standard 8-5 payout.

The 8-5 Payouts

Most machines today, other than the bonus ones we'll discuss later, are 8-5 machines. This is what the pros call machines where the payout is 8 credits for each one credit played when a full house comes up, and 5 credit payouts for each one credit played when a flush is dealt. Let's look at a chart to see what these payouts look like, first with one credit played, and then with five credits wagered.

JACKS OR BETTER
One Credit Bet

Winning Hand	Payout Per Coin
Royal Flush	Progressive or 800
Straight Flush	50
Four of a Kind	25
Full House	8
Flush	5
Straight	4
Three of a Kind	3
Two Pair	2
Jacks or Better	1

The next chart will show the maximum payouts with five credits wagered:

JACKS OR BETTER
5 Credits Bet

Winning Hand	Payout Per Coin
Royal Flush	Progressive or 4,000
Straight Flush	250
Four of a Kind	125
Full House	40
Flush	25
Straight	20
Three of a Kind	15
Two Pair	10
Jacks or Better	5

Always play five coins with Progressive machines. These machines are tied to a bank of machines feeding the progressive jackpot every time a Royal Flush isn't made. The amount the jackpot increases varies, but it slowly but surely builds up from $1,000.

The jackpot total is shown above the bank of machines on a flashing screen that can be seen from quite a distance away in the casino. If you see a screen showing its quarter machines paying off over $2,000, head for them.

Progressive, as well as Flat-Tops, can be played for nickels, quarters or dollars. On a nickel machine, the jackpot starts at $200, while on the dollar machines, it begins at $4,000.

Winning Strategies for the 8-5 Jacks or Better Machines

The following is the correct basic strategy to be played on these machines.

Going For the Royal Flush

Our first goal is to get the Royal Flush, so each time there's a possibility of this occurring, we have to weigh the hands dealt against the chances of drawing to the Royal Flush. Here's our strategy.

1. Whenever we have <u>four cards to a Royal Flush</u>, such as ♥K ♥Q ♥J ♥10, we discard the fifth card, even though it has given us a straight or a flush.

2. In the above example, if there was another King, Queen or Jack, giving us High Pair, we'd discard it, going for the Royal Flush.

3. When we have <u>three to a Royal Flush</u>, we discard a High Pair and draw to the remaining three cards to a Royal. This is in line with our goal of trying to get that Royal Flush whenever possible. For example, we're dealt ♦A ♥A ♥K ♥10 ♠3. We'd go for the three to a Royal Flush in this situation, breaking up the high pair and throwing away the ♦A and ♠3.

However, if we hold the following hands, hands that already have a payout on all cards dealt, we don't go for the Royal Flush.

    a. Straight Flush.

    b. Four of a Kind.

    c. Full House.

    d. Three of a Kind.

4. When holding <u>a small pair (10s or below) and three to a Royal Flush</u>, we discard the pair and go for the Royal Flush.

5. When we have <u>two to a Royal Flush</u>, we hold all pairs over the possibility of going for the Royal Flush. For example, if we hold ♥A ♠A ♦Q and two **rags** (cards that can't help our hand) we retain the Aces rather than retaining the two high diamonds. If we hold a low pair and two to the Royal, we still hold onto the low pair, and discard the two cards to the Royal.

6. With <u>two to a Royal,</u> we hold onto four flushes and four straights, three of a kind and two pair, rather than going for the Royal Flush.

7. If we have <u>two to a Royal</u> and another high card, but no pair, we discard the other high card. *This is an important move that should always be made.* For example, suppose we're dealt ♣Q ♦A ♦K and two rags. We discard the ♣Q and the two rags, going for the Royal with our A and K of diamonds. I have personally hit two Royals this way.

So, always keep that Royal Flush in mind. It gives us the really big payout, and it's always lurking in the machine. We can't pass up the opportunity to go for it when the situation favors us.

Straight Flushes, Flushes & Straights

Our best payout, other than the Royal Flush, is the Straight Flush. However, its' payout is merely 50 for 1 or 250 credits, against the Royal Flush's payoff of 4,000 credits or the big Progressive Jackpot. Therefore, although we're likely to get a Straight Flush four times as often as a Royal Flush, the payout is only 1/16 of the Royal Flush, and even less if a Progressive Jackpot hits.

Although we must be aware of the Straight Flush, it's not something we're constantly looking for, as in the case of the Royal.

When we are dealt a Flush, and it contains four to a Straight Flush, such as ♥10 ♥9 ♥8 ♥7 ♥2, our best play is to retain the Flush and not go for the Straight Flush. However, if we are dealt a Straight, and it contains four cards to a

Straight Flush within it, we discard the odd card and go for the Straight Flush. An example might be ♠7 ♠6 ♠5 ♠4 ♦3. We kiss off the ♦3.

A High Pair is always preferable to a four to a Flush or Straight. We retain the High Pair (Jacks or Better) and break up the possible Flush or Straight.

With a low pair, we break up the low pair (10s or lower) in favor of the four to a Flush, but we retain the low pair and break up the four to a Straight.

Four of a Kinds, Full Houses & Three of a Kinds

Four of a Kind hands pay half of what Straight Flushes pay, but occur much more frequently, about once in every 420 hands, or about 22.7 times more frequently than the Straight Flush. Since it pays half of what the Straight Flush pays, it's a much better value for us, coming up so frequently.

Sometimes, Four of a Kind hands come out of the blue and surprise us. We start with a lowly pair of 3s and two more 3s come on the screen. Or we may stay with a Three of a Kind hand and get the fourth of that rank. Sometimes, we'll really be surprised by staying with but one high card and getting three more for a Four of a Kind hand!

This is the main difference between regular Draw Poker and Video Poker. In the regular game, we wouldn't stay in with low pairs or just one high card, because it'll be a loser in the long run. In Video Poker we have nothing to lose, for we've already invested our money.

Three of a Kind hands occur about once every thirteen times, or about 7.5% of the time. We may get them by being dealt them outright, and drawing to a retained pair. Or perhaps if we're fortunate, we've stayed in with one high card and received two more of the same rank.

We always stay for the draw with a Three of a Kind hand. It's much stronger for us than three to a Royal Flush, so, if we're dealt ♥K ♥Q ♥10 ♠10 ♦10, we retain the three 10s and discard the K and Q of hearts.

A Full House if sometimes made from a Three of a Kind hand, where the odds are roughly 11-1 against this happening. Of course, like all hands in Video Poker, a Full House can come out of the blue, where we've retained one low pair, such as ♦5 ♠5 and see the screen fill up with ♦J ♠J ♥J.

A Full House occurs a little over 1% of the time.

Two Pair, High Pairs & Low Pairs

Two Pair occur about once every 7.6 hands and pays off with only two credits for each credit invested, or in reality, at even-money. Thus, we get back 10 credits for the five credits played; the five we invested plus the five won. When we have two pair, we go for the Full House by dumping the odd card, although the odds are about 10-1 against this happening.

A High Pair allows us to get our original investment back. Although this doesn't sound like much, it is the reason for the game's popularity, since it enables players to constantly get payouts and thus retain their bankroll till the big payouts come through. We should be dealt a High Pair about once every 4.6 hands.

We retain the High Pair when it is part of a possible Straight or Flush, and discard the other cards in those situations. If the High Pair is part of a Straight Flush, such as ♦J ♦10 ♦9 ♦8 ♠J, then we get rid of the ♠J and go for the Straight Flush. We also do this even if the possible Straight Flush can be made by drawing to it as an inside Straight Flush, as in the following situation:

♥Q ♥J ♥10 ♥8 ♠Q

In the above example, the ♠Q would be discarded. There's a chance for a Straight Flush, a Flush, a Straight and another High Pair when this is done, giving us more powerful hands to go for, with bigger payouts.

With small pairs, we have hands that can give us many payouts when they are improved. Normally in regular draw poker, only a very weak player would retain a pair of 4s, but in Video Poker, those 4s can turn into Three of a Kind hands or better if we get a lucky draw.

We retain the small pairs when we have three rags in the same hand, or in the following hand:

$$♥A ♠K ♥J ♠5 ♦5$$

We hold onto the 5s and discard the three High cards. We also retain the small pair in a Four Straight hand, but get rid of them in a Four Flush hand. If they are part of a three to a Straight Flush, such as ♦8 ♦7 ♦6 ♠6 ♥K, we retain the small pair of 6s.

Other Hands

Most of the time, the hands dealt to you before the draw won't be winners by themselves. You'll have to improve them to get a payout. At times, you'll find yourself with a powerful drawing hand that comes up empty. For example:

$$♠A ♠Q ♠K ♠J ♦3$$

Having four to a Royal Flush, we discard

the ♦ 3 and hit the Draw button, hoping for the **BIG ONE!** Instead we're dealt the 9 of hearts and end up without a payout of any kind. Other good hands will end up as blanks for us. This is to be expected. Don't get discouraged. There will b other times, as there was for this author, when the following hand was dealt to him.

♦4   ♥7   ♦9   ♠2   ♥J

Faced with this pile of garbage I retained the Jack of hearts, the only viable play. Imagine my surprise when I drew four cards and saw the following on the screen:

♥K   ♥Q   ♥10   ♥A   ♥J
HELD

And on the screen were these words:
WINNER! JACKPOT! ROYAL FLUSH!

How sweet it was!

Many times we'll get a hand like this:

♦4   ♥A   ♠J   ♣6   ♥3

We hold the Ace and the Jack, for we're trying to pair one of these to get at least five credits. Many players make the mistake of retaining only the Ace and discarding the Jack. That's a bad play. Hold onto both. Remember, in Video Poker, any High Card that is paired will pay off. In this regard, an Ace is no stronger than a Jack.

We already have discussed holding four to a Straight Flush (whether open-ended or gut shot) four to a Flush and four to a Straight. If you're dealt three to a Straight Flush, discard the rags and go for it. If the hand contains a High Card as part of the Straight Flush, it is that much stronger, such as ♦J ♦10 ♦9, since the Jack may be paired even if you miss any other hand after the draw.

With low pairs, we retain them in the hope of getting a monster hand, such as Four of a Kind, or any payout. Suppose we see ♣5 ♦5 ♥A ♣J ♦10. Here, we hold the pair of 5s. Lots of times we won't improve, but there will be times when we get a good payout for this play. Now let's deal with those hands that are so bad there's no reason to hold any of the cards. When we get five **blanks** or rags, we hold nothing and go for five new cards on the draw. Such a hand might be:

♥2 ♦6 ♣10 ♦8 ♥4

There's nothing worth holding. To get five new cards, simply press the Deal/Draw button and five new cards will appear on the screen. Don't be afraid to get rid of all five cards. As the poker pros say "muck them." There's always a chance of getting a payoff of some kind. The biggest one I ever got after mucking the five cards were four 6s. And by some miracle, you might even get a Royal Flush doing this!

Some Winning Hints

One of the important differences between regular Draw Poker and Video Poker is this – when you play Draw Poker you're able to sort your cards in the proper order. If you've been dealt a pair, you put them side by side. If you have been dealt four to a Straight, you place those cards in their proper sequence.

However, when playing Video Poker, the cards come up on the screen just as the computer deals them and the player must carefully see just what has been dealt. So you have to be super-careful about not overlooking a strong hand. Most machines will immediately show what you have, by changing color on one of the lines.

For example, if the payout lines are in yellow, the line showing the winning hand will appear in white. If you've been dealt Two Pair, for example, that line will change color. But many players play the game at a rapid pace and sometimes overlook this indication.

I watched a player muck these cards before the draw:

♦5   ♥6   ♣3   ♦2   ♠4

He simply overlooked the straight. Another player, dealt a wheel (a Straight from Ace to 5) retained only the Ace and overlooked his made Straight.

Therefore, my best advice is to slow down a bit and examine the cards that have been dealt to you at the outset, and see just what you have on the screen.

Take your time in determining the correct play. If you do make a mistake and hold the wrong card, you can rectify that mistake by pressing the Hold button again, negating the previous hold. As long as you don't press the Deal/Draw button, you still have a chance to make any changes necessary.

Even experienced veterans of the game make mistakes. They may be weary or tired or upset, and they can, in this state, overlook obvious plays. If you reach a point where the game has become tedious, leave the machine and cash in. Take a break and go back another time when you're refreshed and ready to play.

A final note: when playing progressive machines, avoid those with payouts that indicate the Jackpot has recently been hit. The progressives start at $1,000 and if you're in a casino where the payouts are $1,092 and $1,100, don't play these machines. You want to play those that haven't been hit for awhile.

Practicing at Home

In earlier editions of this book, I suggested practicing at home by dealing out cards by hand. But now, if you have a computer, the best way to practice is to buy software that contains Video Poker and other casino games, and play on your computer. There is generally an "expert advice" section on these games. Cardoza Publishing makes a fine software program which I highly recommend.

At home, you should make sure that you have the basic strategy of the game down pat. If you make a mistake it won't cost you money. You'll learn fast this way, and using this book as a guide, you'll easily become an expert player. After you're comfortable with the game and know what you're doing, you can go to a casino and play for real money.

4. Testing Your Knowledge Of Jacks Or Better

The following is a small quiz to refine and test your knowledge of the game played in the casino. We'll assume that we're at a machine that has an 8-5 payout on the Full House and Flush, respectively. Decide how to play each of the following hands:

1. ♣5 ♦5 ♠A ♥9 ♦10
We hold the pair of 5s and discard the other cards. We never save a "kicker" such as the Ace in Video Poker.

2. ♦9 ♦K ♣K ♦9 ♦2
We hold the Kings and discard the other diamonds. Always hold the High Pair as opposed to drawing for a possible Flush.

3. ♠K ♠Q ♠A ♠10 ♥J
With four to the Royal Flush, we discard the heart Jack. Whenever we have four to a Royal, we're going for the Jackpot.

4. ♠Q ♦3 ♠J ♥K ♥2

This kind of hand comes up frequently. We retain the Queen and Jack of spades, and kiss off the other cards. We can possibly make a Royal Flush here, and don't want the King of hearts in the way.

5. ♠9 ♥5 ♥2 ♥8 ♣3

There is nothing worthwhile in this pile of junk. Even though we have three to a Flush in hearts, there's no reason to overcome the great odds of drawing to it. We're better off going for five fresh cards after the draw.

6. ♠10 ♣8 ♦3 ♠J ♠4

At first glance, it would seem correct to hold the spade Jack and discard the other cards. Or we could go for a long shot and hold all three spades. Both of these decisions are incorrect. We hold the Jack and 10 of spades, giving us two to a Royal.

7. ♠2 ♥A ♣K ♦J ♣2

We hold the deuces and discard the three High Cards. A small pair is powerful in Video Poker, because it can improve dramatically, even to a Four of a Kind hand. In this instance we don't chase a possible pairing of a High Card, and we don't hold kickers.

8. ♥Q ♦J ♠10 ♠4 ♠3

We have both a three to a Flush and a Straight. However, we also have a Queen and Jack, which, if either is paired, will get us five credits. We therefore hold the Queen and Jack and discard the other cards.

9. ♦J ♦K ♠9 ♦Q ♥9

We have three to a Royal Flush plus a small pair of 9s. We get rid of a small pair in this situation and go for the Royal.

10. ♥K ♥Q ♥J ♥A ♥5

Here we have four to a Royal and a formed Flush. In this situation, we get rid of the heart 5 and go for the Royal. Why? Just look at the odds. Suppose the Progressive payout at this point is $1,600. When we put in $1.25, our payout is 1,280 for 1. Now, if we get rid of the 5 of hearts, our chances of getting the Royal is only 46-1 to get a payment of 1,280 for 1. We'll take that any day of the week.

Well, that's our quiz. Just a representative number of questions, but of course, there is much more to the game. My suggestion: if you want to learn Video Poker so you can play on a professional level and actually have an edge over the casino, buy the excellent advanced strategy available in the back of this book.

5. Bonus, Double Bonus & Double Double Bonus

In recent years, new forms of Video Poker have sprung up, and some of the more common games are known as Bonus games, either single, double or double double.

You can find these games in practically all casinos, and they may be found as individual Video Poker games, or as part of a Multi-Poker format, where the casino or store or whatever allows you to touch the screen and pick the game of your choice.

Also, Game King™ machines, manufactured by IGT, give you a choice of the same games. If you want to change games, all you have to do is press a button which says "more games" or "other games" and once more you'll see the screen in order to make a new selection.

Some of these games have progressive jackpots, while most are of the flat-top variety with a fixed payout of 4,000 credits or coins if the jackpot is hit with the player wagering five credits or coins and getting a Royal Flush.

Many of the Multi-Poker machines can be paid off by coins or by a ticket, which is brought to the change cashier. Of course, jackpots are paid off by a casino employee at the machine, with cash.

Here is a typical payout schedule for a Bonus Poker machine.

BONUS POKER PAYOUTS
Five Credits Bet

Winning Hand	Payout Per Coin
Royal Flush	4,000 or Progressive
Straight Flush	250
Four Aces	400
Four 2s, 3s or 4s	200
Four 5s through Kings	125
Full House	35
Flush	25
Three of a Kind	15
Two Pair	10
Jacks of Better	5

We can immediately ascertain the differences between these payouts and those of ordinary 8-5 Jacks or Better machines. First of all, this is a 7-5 machine, with only 35 credits for a Full House.

The bonus feature is in the payouts for Four Aces and Four 2s, 3s and 4s. A normal

Jacks or Better machine pays all Four of a Kind hand with 125 credits. Here, with four Aces, the payout is 400 credits or 3.2 times the ordinary payout. And the four 2s, 3s or 4s are paid off with 200 credits, or 1.6 times the ordinary payout.

With these payouts in mind, we must alter our basic strategy when playing the bonus machine. First of all, if we have an Ace and another High Card of a different suit dealt to us, we retain just the Ace. We would also retain a pair of 2s through 4s, rather than discarding them going for a Flush.

If possible, play the Progressive Bonus machines, if you can find them. Knowing the popularity of Video Poker, the manufacturers and casinos have gone more and more to Flat-Tops, with a standard 4,000 credit or coin payout. In the early days of Video Poker, there were plenty of progressive machines, with some great payouts. But there harder to find, and this penalizes the player.

At first glance, the Double Bonus seems a much better deal for the player than the Bonus Poker machine. Payouts for Four of a Kind hands are double those in the Bonus Poker ones. And this is a 9-6 machine (payouts on the Full House and Flush) rather than a 7-5 machine.

DOUBLE BONUS PAYOUTS
Five Credits Bet

Winning Hand	Payout Per Coin
Royal Flush	4,000 or Progressive
Straight Flush	250
Four Aces	800
Four 2, 3s or 4s	400
Four 5s through Kings	250
Full House	45
Flush	30
Straight	20
Three of a Kind	15
Two Pair	5
Jacks or Better	5

The rub is the payout for the Two Pair, which is even-money, rather than 2 for 1. Does this make a difference? It certainly does, for Two Pair hands normally occur every 7.6 hands. Getting the smaller payout makes a tremendous difference, for the small payouts is what keeps us in the game, and keeps our bankroll fresh.

When playing these Double Bonus machines, again we focus on getting the Four of a Kind hands, especially the Aces, with its' $200 payoff on a quarter machine.

With an Ace and another big card of a different suit, we retain only the Ace. With the

2s, 3s and 4s, these small pairs can give us $100 if they develop into Four of a Kind hands, and so, when we have a four flush, and a pair of 2s, 3s or 4s, we save the small pair, and don't go for the Flush. In fact, with any pair, it is favored over the possible Flush, and certainly over the possible Straight.

If we're dealt Two Pair at the outset, we retain only the High Pair (Jacks or Better) and discard the smaller ones in a hand such as Q Q 6 6. It's approximately 10-1 against getting the Full House, and generally we'll be only getting our even-money payout after the draw.

With the High Pair, we can improve to a big Four of a Kind payout, while still guaranteeing the even-money payout for Jacks or Better.

This machine following is an 8-5 machine, with only even-money payouts for Two Pair hands. The dazzling payout of 2,000 credits or coins for Four Aces with a 2, 3 or 4 is quite seductive here, as is the 800 credit payout for Four Aces, or for Four 2s, 3s, 4s with an Ace, 2, 3 or 4. Here's what this means. Suppose you are extremely lucky and are dealt the following hand at the outset:

♣A ♠A ♦A ♥A ♦8

With an ordinary Jacks or Better machine, you'd press **HELD** under all the cards, and get your payout. But not here. You must get rid of the ♦8 and hold the aces. If you're fortunate enough to get a 2, 3 or 4 of any suit, you'd receive a payout of 2,000 credits ($500) instead of 800 credits ($200). You must be alert to this when playing the Double Double Bonus machines.

DOUBLE DOUBLE BONUS
Five Credits Bet

Winning Hand	Payout Per Coin
Royal Flush	4,000 or Progressive
Straight Flush	250
Four Aces with a 2, 3 or 4	2,000
Four Aces	800
Four 2s, 3s or 4s with A, 2, 3, 4	800
Four 2s, 3s or 4s	400
Four 5s through Kings	250
Full House	40
Flush	25
Straight	20
Three of a Kind	15
Two Pair	5
Jacks or Better	5

The same principle holds true when dealt four 2s, 3s or 4s at the outset. You must kiss off the odd card unless it's an Ace, 2, 3 or 4, and try to double your credits from 400 to 800.

With a Double Double Bonus machine, you'll find your money draining away unless you can hit one of the big hands. The even-money for Two Pair and the 8-5 payout for the Full House and Flush penalize the player otherwise.

Triple Play and Five Play Machines

These machines are somewhat popular because they allow a player to gamble at either three or five Video Poker games at the same time. With Triple Play, one open hand is shown on the screen, and the player holds those cards that will give him the biggest possible payout. This is done on the bottom or "A" line.

For example, he might hold two Kings, and thus each of the three hands will show the two Kings. Then he draws three cards to each of the hands to improve. With big hands there are triple payouts, but of course, if his or her luck goes badly, the losses mount rapidly, because fifteen coins or credits are being bet at one time for the maximum payouts.

With Five Play, five hands are played this way, and that means twenty-five coins or credits bet at one time. These machines are built to be bet with either nickels, dimes, quarters or half-dollars. No coins need be used, for credits will be awarded after a bill is slipped into the machine.

The Triple Play and Five Play payouts are pretty much the same, with maximum 4,000 credit payouts. The following chart will show them for a Bonus machine.

TRIPLE PLAY & FIVE PLAY BONUS PAYOUTS Five Credits Bet	
Winning Hand	**Payout Per Coin**
Royal Flush	4,000
Straight Flush	250
Four Aces	400
Four 2s 3s or 4s	200
Four 5s through Kings	125
Full House	40
Flush	25
Straight	20
Three of a Kind	15
Two Pair	10
Jacks or Better	5

These 8-5 machines without a progressive jackpot are not recommended for play except for those who want to do some gambling, in the hope of getting some big payouts paid three or five times at once.

6. Deuces Wild

Like the other versions of Video Poker, Deuces Wild is played with an ordinary 52-card deck. However, each of the four deuces (2s) is a **wild card**, which means it can be used as any card in the deck, not only in rank (such as the K or Q, for example) but as any suit. Since there are four deuces in the deck, hands containing at least one deuce have been calculated to occur about 35% of the time.

Note that the weakest possible hand with a payout is Three of a Kind. And a Five of a Kind hand pays only 15 for 1! That's a pretty shabby payoff. With the deuces running wild in the deck, all kinds of crazy hands can be made and a lot of the payouts are penalized, especially for the weaker hands.

Playing Deuces Wild can be a roller coaster ride with wild streaks coming and going, both favorable and unfavorable. When the deuces show up on the screen, all kinds of payouts are possible. When they're absent, it's a desert out there, because of the low payouts on relatively strong hands, such as even-money on a Three of a Kind hand.

Even when dealt one deuce, your chances of making a hand that pays out is only 54%. When you're dealt three deuces, you're assured of at least a Four of a Kind hand, but even this pays only 20 credits.

The following chart shows the payout schedule for Deuces Wild Video Poker.

DEUCES WILD PAYOUT Five Credits Bet	
Winning Hand	**Payout Per Coin**
Royal Flush (no 2s)	4,000 or Progressive
Four Deuces	1,000
Royal Flush with Deuce	100
Five of a Kind	60
Straight Flush	45
Four of a Kind	20
Full House	20
Flush	15
Straight	10
Three of a Kind	5

Deuces Wild Strategy

1. If we have three deuces and two to a Royal Flush, that's a Royal Flush and should be held intact.

2. With two deuces and three to a Royal, this hand should be held intact as a Royal Flush.

3. Two deuces and a Three of a Kind hand is a Five of a Kind hand and should be held intact.

4. If we have two deuces and three cards to a Straight Flush, this hand should be held intact. If it's merely a flush, save the two deuces.

5. With two deuces and three odd cards, none of which can give you a Royal Flush, draw three cards to the deuces.

6. With a single deuce and three to a Royal Flush, plus an odd card, we discard the odd card and draw one card.

7. Without a deuce, if the hand gives us a payout with all five cards intact, we hold the hand and don't draw.

8. Without a deuce, we hold the following hands: four to a Straight Flush, four to a Flush and four to a Straight, discarding the odd card.

9. Without a deuce, we hold three card Straight Flushes and draw.

10. With hands such as ♦A ♥K ♠Q ♦4 ♥8, we discard all the cards.

Pairing any of the big cards or even making two pair gives us nothing. You'll find you'll often, up to 25% of the time, be discarding the cards dealt to you.

Play the game correctly, and you'll be rewarded with all kinds of big hands, and if you encounter a good winning streak, this game can earn you some good money even without hitting the Royal Flush.

7. Jokers Wild

This game is played often on a nickel or quarter machine and some IGT machines call it "Joker Poker." The single Joker in the deck is a wild card and can be used for any ranked card or suit to make the best possible poker hand. The following chart shows a typical payout schedule for the quarter game.

JOKERS WILD PAYOUT
Five Credits Bet

Winning Hand	Payout Per Coin
Royal Flush	4,000 or Progressive
Five of a Kind	1,000 or Progressive
Royal Flush with Joker	500
Straight Flush	250
Four of a Kind	75
Full House	35
Flush	25
Straight	15
Three of a Kind	10
Two Pair	5
Kings or Better	5

With the addition of the Joker, we now have a deck containing 53 cards, with approximately 10% more different kinds of hands dealt out than in the 52-card standard Video Poker games.

The lack of payout below a pair of Kings makes this machine a tough one to beat. When the Joker doesn't appear at the outset, before the draw, there are going to be many hands that will not get any payout whatsoever.

Joker Wild: Kings or Better Strategy

The Joker will appear in the hand less than 10% of the time, or about 9.4%. Many times, without the Joker, we'll simply have to discard all five cards dealt at the outset. Since only Aces and Kings are good as High Pairs, we don't retain a Queen or Jack. They're as useless as an odd 9 or 4.

• We will break up a formed Straight to go for a Straight Flush, if no Joker has been dealt at the outset. Among hands to be discarded whole before the draw are the following:

• Two cards to a Flush.

• Three cards to a Flush, unless it gives us a chance at a Royal Flush, such as A J 10 suited, or 9 7 6 suited.

• With the Joker present, there is a good chance to get a Straight Flush, and we get rid of a completed Flush in a hand such as this, to go for the Straight Flush.

Jkr ♥6 ♥7 ♥5 ♥Q

With the above hand, we dump the Queen of hearts and draw one card. When we have three to a Straight Flush with the Joker, as above, we retain these four cards and get rid of a high card, going for the Straight Flush rather than being satisfied with a High Pair payout.

• When dealt the Joker at the outset, we'll retain only the Joker if the hand has two cards other than the Joker, for a flush. And the same is true if there's no chance for a Royal Flush.

• Hands to hold are Three of a Kind, Straights and Flushes, formed before the draw.

Joker Wild is a complicated game, and is best studied at home without money, by using software on your computer or dealing out hands with a joker in the deck. Unless you feel comfortable with the game, I'd stick to simpler Video Poker versions.

8. Money Management

The Bankroll

You should feel comfortable financially and emotionally playing Video Poker machines because you may find yourself losing at the outset. Unless you get some big hands, the money in your possession may just dribble away.

I would start with $20 on the nickel machines, $100 on the quarter machines and $300 on the dollar machines. If any of these bankrolls will hurt you financially, don't gamble on Video Poker.

Practically all machines now take bills, and some tickets that can be used in lieu of cash. Most machines still pay out in coins, so make certain that you have a bucket nearby to use when you cash out. Don't leave the machine either with credits on it or coins in the well. Ring the bell for service and have a casino employee bring you one of the casino's paper buckets.

When to Quit

A gambling principle well worth memorizing is this- *the first loss is the cheapest*.

If you lose your initial bankroll, don't start looking for an ATM machine. Stop playing. The machine has been cruel to you, and enough is enough. There are other machines that will be kind; that will give you constant payouts and some big ones at that. There's nothing sweeter, other than hitting the Royal Flush, to keep getting Full Houses and Four of a Kind hands, with the credits mounting up into the high 100s.

But no matter how many credits you have, make sure to cash out. You will either get coins or a printed ticket which will say "Cash-Out" and show the name of the casino, the date, the amount of the ticket in terms of cash, and a notice that it expires in 60 days.

What you don't want to do is have a big win, a ton of credits, and then watch the machine turn sour and those credits evaporate. Make a mind decision to get away as a winner. Suppose you're ahead 380 credits on a quarter machine. 300 credits add up to $75. If you go down that far, cash out. I've seen players lose their 380 credits, take more money from their wallets and end up with a frightening loss. *Leave a winner*, if possible.

Sometime a machine will fool you. I was in a downtown Las Vegas casino and had the choice of two quarter machines, the end one or the one next to it. I was waiting for a friend to take to lunch, and figured I'd take a shot with $20. It was a progressive paying about $1,600. As I stood there, a middle-aged man took the end machine, so I sat down at the other one and slid in the $20 bill.

My neighbor chuckled as he was dealt a Full House. I got zilch. Then he got another Full House. I was rewarded with nothing. He followed this with a Flush, then Three of a Kind and another Full House. I looked at my watch. I had about five minutes to go before my friend would show up. And was down to 10 credits. Well, there went the $20, I thought, and then the following hand was dealt:

♦A ♠Q ♦10 ♥5 ♥4

I saved the Ace and 10 of diamonds. Instinctively I always go for the possible Royal. As my neighbor hit a Straight, I tapped the Deal/Draw button and looked at the screen: **A Royal Flush! WINNER!**

There was this beautiful hand showing:

♦A ♦K ♦10 ♦J ♦Q
HELD   HELD

A casino employee paid me off just as my friend arrived for lunch. I wished my neighbor good luck and we were on our way to a buffet lunch, which the casino comped without me asking.

9. Glossary of Video Poker

Bonus Poker – A form of Jacks or Better where bonuses are paid for certain dealt hands.

Cash Out Button – A button that releases all the credits and drops all previously won coins into the well. On some modern machines, a ticket showing the cash value of the credits is issued.

Cash Out Ticket – A ticket issued by the machine showing the cash value of the credits. This machine can be used on other machines in lieu of bills.

Cashier Cage – A place on the casino floor where players can receive cash for their coins or cash-out tickets.

Changeperson – A casino employee who makes change and roams through the casino floor for this purpose. With the advent of machines that accept bills and tickets, changepersons are becoming obsolete.

Credit/Max Credit Button – The Credit button, when pressed, plays one credit at a time. The Max Credit button plays five credits or whatever the maximum bet is.

Deal/Draw Button – This button, when pressed, causes the machine to issue a new hand if fewer than the maximum credits have been bet. It is also used, when the maximum credits are bet, to issue cards after the draw.

Deuces Wild – A form of Video Poker where each of the four 2s are wild cards.

Double Bonus/Double Double Bonus Poker – Forms of Video Poker where bonuses are paid for certain dealt hands such as Four Aces.

Five of a Kind – This hand is possible when playing a wild card game, such as Deuces Wild or Jokers Wild.

Five Play Machine – A machine that plays five hands of Video Poker at the same time.

Flattop Machines – These machines have a fixed maximum payout for a Royal Flush, usually 4,000 credits or coins.

Four Flush – A hand consisting of four cards of the same suit, together with an odd card. Example- ♠4 ♠9 ♠10 ♠K ♦5

Four of a Kind – A hand consisting of four cards of the same rank such as 9 9 9 9.

Four Straight – A hand consisting of four cards, not of the same suit, but in sequence, such as ♦3 ♥4 ♠5 ♠6 together with an odd card. This is also known as an open-ended straight.

Full House – A hand that consists of a pair and

three of a kind, such as 8 8 J J J.

Gutshot Straight – A hand consisting of four cards to a possible straight, needing an interior card to form the straight, such as ♣8 ♦9 ♠J ♦Q.

High Card – A Jack, Queen, King or Ace, which, if paired in Jacks or Better and some other Video Poker games, will pay back the original bet to the player.

Hold Button – A button that, if pressed, will hold a particular card to the original hand dealt, so that it won't be replaced by the draw.

Jokers Wild – A form of Video Poker that has a Joker in addition to the regular 52-card deck. The Joker is a wild card in this game.

Kicker – A high, odd card which is held before the draw. An example might be an Ace held with a pair of 3s. Not recommended in Video Poker.

Low Pair – A pair, usually 10s or lower ranked cards, which doesn't qualify for a payout in Jacks or Better poker.

Mechanic, Slots Mechanic – A casino employee who repairs any machine that is broken.

Multi-Play Machine – A machine which offers a number of Video Poker games. The player chooses his or her game by touching the game shown on the screen.

Original Hand – The first five cards dealt to a player before he or she draws cards to improve the hand.

Progressive Machines – Video Poker machines whose Jackpot is not fixed, but increases each time a Royal Flush isn't hit.

Rags/Blanks – Cards that are useless in forming a particular poker hand.

Royal Flush – The best hand in video poker; consists of the Ace, King, Queen, Jack and 10 of the same suit.

Straight – Five cards in consecutive sequence but not of the same suit, such as 7, 8, 9, 10 and Jack. Also A, 2, 3, 4 and 5 as well as 10, Jack, Queen, King and Ace.

Straight Flush – Five cards in sequence and of the same suit but without an Ace, such as ♦7 ♦8 ♦9 ♦10 ♦Jack.

Three of a Kind – A hand consisting of three cards of the same rank, such as 4 4 4, together with two odd cards.

Triple Play – A form of Video Poker in which three hands are bet and played at the same time.

Two Pair – A hand consisting of two separate pairs, such as K K 5 5, together with an odd card.

Well – The metal area in the bottom of the machine to which paid out coins fall.

Win at Blackjack Without Counting Cards!

Breakthrough in Blackjack!!!
The Cardoza 1,2,3 Non-Counter Strategy

Beat Multiple Deck Blackjack Without Counting Cards!

You heard right! Now, for the **first time** ever, **win** at multiple deck blackjack **without counting cards**! Until I developed the Cardoza Multiple Deck Non-Counter (The 1,2,3 Strategy), I thought it was impossible. Don't be intimidated anymore by 4, 6 or 8 deck games - now *you* have the **advantage**!

Exciting Strategy - Anyone Can Win!

We're **excited** about this strategy for it allows anyone at all to **have the advantage** over any casino in the world in a multiple deck game. You don't need a great memory, you don't count cards, you don't need to be good at math - you only need to know the **winning secrets** of the Cardoza Multiple Deck Non-Counter and use but a **little effort** to be a **winner**.

Simple But Effective - Be a Leisurely Winner!

This strategy is so **simple**, yet so **effective**, you will be amazed. With a **minimum of effort**, this remarkable strategy, which we also call the 1,2,3 (as easy as 1,2,3), allows you to **win** without studiously following cards. Drink, converse, whatever - they'll never suspect that you can **beat the casino**!

Not as powerful as a card counting strategy, but **powerful enough to make you a winner** - with the odds!!!

Extra Bonus!

Complete listing of all options and variations at blackjack and how they affect the player. ($5 Value!) **Extra, Extra Bonus!!** Not really a bonus for we could not sell you the strategy without protecting you against gettting barred. The 1,000 word essay, "How to Disguise the Fact That You're an Expert," and 1,500 word "How Not To Get Barred," are also included free. ($15 Value)

To Order, send ~~$75~~ $50 by check or money order to <u>Cardoza Publishing</u>

PROFESSIONAL VIDEO POKER STRATEGY
Win at Video Poker - With the Odds!

At last, for the **first time,** and for **serious players only,** the GRI **Professional Video Poker** strategy is released so you too can play to win! **You read it right** - this strategy gives you the **mathematical advantage** over the casino and what's more, it's **easy to learn!**

PROFESSIONAL STRATEGY SHOWS YOU HOW TO WIN WITH THE ODDS
This **powerhouse strategy,** played for **big profits** by an **exclusive** circle of **professionals,** people who make their living at the machines, is now made available to you! You too can win - with the odds - and this **winning strategy** shows you how!

HOW TO PLAY FOR A PROFIT
You'll learn the **key factors** to play on a **pro level:** which machines will turn you a profit, break-even and win rates, hands per hour and average win per hour charts, time value, team play and more! You'll also learn big play strategy, alternate jackpot play, high and low jackpot play and key strategies to follow.

WINNING STRATEGIES FOR ALL MACHINES
This **comprehensive, advanced pro package** not only shows you how to win money at the 8-5 progressives, but also, the **winning strategies** for 10s or better, deuces wild, joker's wild, flat-top, progressive and special options features.

BE A WINNER IN JUST ONE DAY
In just one day, after learning our strategy, you will have the skills to **consistently win money** at video poker - with the odds. The strategies are easy to use under practical casino conditions.

BONUS - PROFESSIONAL PROFIT EXPECTANCY FORMULA ($15 VALUE)
For serious players, we're including this bonus essay which discusses the profit expectancy principles of video poker and how to relate them to real dollars and cents in your game.

To order, send $50 by check or money order to <u>Cardoza Publishing</u>
